MFA Monthly
NO. 2

MFA Monthly
VOLUME 1, NO. 2

November 2012

Editor	Chris Pappas
Fiction	Elizabeth Quinn
Poetry	Amy King
Essay	Chris Wong
Cover Art	Barrett Travis
Fiction Editor	Christopher Murphy

© 2012 by USPOCO BOOOKS

Please contact the editors at uspocobooks@gmail.com to request permission, if you wish to reproduce any portion of this issue for any reason. Reproduction of any portion of this text, or of the text in whole, is otherwise prohibited.

MFA Monthly

NO. 2

VOLUME 1

MFA Monthly
is produced and published by USPOCO BOOKS,
in partnership with
ManuFacturedArtists.com.

Submissions

Submissions are read year round. We only guarantee a response if accepted. After three weeks, if you have not heard from our staff, you may inquire via one email on the status of a submitted work.

Send your original and unpublished work (three to nine pages of poetry, one story or one essay) to uspocobooks@gmail.com. Simultaneous submissions are fine, of course.

Send cover submissions of original art or photography as an image file of at least 300 DPI. Keep in mind that this a pocket-sized magazine with dimensions of about 5 X 7 inches.

Include month, genre and author's name in the subject line. Submissions may also be considered for publication @ ManuFacturedArtists.com, a blog of the arts.

Do not include contributor notes or bios, for we do not publish them.

We only accept email submissions. Each contributor will receive five free copies of the magazine. USPOCO BOOKS will ship your contributor's copies to any five addresses in the continental US. Additional copies may be purchased at Amazon.com, uspoco.com or your local independent bookstore. Ask your local bookstore to carry USPOCO magazines and books!

MFA Monthly

NO. 2

USPOCO BOOKS
Dallas

five poems

Amy King

THE WOMAN, YOU

Asks of the omelet made with human hair
to dye tapioca the same shade as caviar.
Women in Mexico pass mirrors unnoticed.
The woman with horsehair hovers
in the hem of her own invisible cloak.
Her framework holds vases of tequila
with children riding horses
like animals romping on a wooden carpet.
Their hoofs echo trees lost at root.
God my guts keep bellowing, she seizes.

Yes, let's, echoes the sound of Creation's
birds taking place in the fleshly room
found in the same home
of the hem on the skirt of a female figure
painted by birds on the wall that holds her fresco.
They come to life on paper and flit
through the window, and out.
Thus the scene of a lonely woman, a lovely woman,
traps passersby in the Geranium Estate's
highest tower, caring alone for cageling moons.

SEED BOMBING

Maternity marries a landscape
mummified by children.
As a debutante, she stood lounging
up at the light
that falls behind the lines
soldiering men who shoot
pellets into abdomens. She fashions
fallout long before
it's fashionable to defend.
With photographs of dolls,
the Leonardos pose
alone in their grins.
Their architecture rises,
closes the story of humans
called Mythography.
The cuts crawl deep
with their oldest friends,
flailing the ages of death
gases and seasons.
The grass lies down,
quietly feral.
With faces cracked
by a fractured pavement,
the future open only
to reflection's post-mortem
cancers. They also come up
through the cracks.
They say you can see ghosts
in your reflection.
For the moon's silhouette,
her skirts rustle

with nether regions of those
with no whistle, no war,
no house, but a home
where they bury the children.

LADY BABA & THE FORTY THIEVES

Photos of Nazis make no sense anymore.
Neither do films or their ilk today.
I don't know what to do with them either,
so I hold out my hands, open-
palmed and cross
myself out to become my own lover,
Lady Baba of the Otherworld.
I'm full body doping now, the inner elbow
of the open-world creases, and I'll play temporary
with dreamwood. Float down like cork,
a padded song to the tune of a liberation quote
to keep paddling wherever the shore rearviews me.
People will note my U.S. Citizen initiative
as the innovative fixture of the future,
how we will be on just this side of nearly enough,
but not quite – what kind?
Relevant beacons and that Diane di Prima poem
on how the only war is against the imagination,
as if we know how to be against anything at all?
I thought of something that might fit:
Lady Baba is another discipline entirely,
not ancient or ritual or titular, but more capable
of subterfuge via the discarded, the grey and brittle
that passes for nothing in total, a bag of fragile
bones and weak lungs barely breathing,
except to take up small seats on buses and subways
without anyone noticing their own weight or what
the feeble hide-away from the light of day.
Less for the sum of pieces that come together,
the eventual passing of old ladies,
minor chess moves

in the neighboring town of the Netherworld.
It's our turn to dismantle disciples,
to fuck with machines that render from clay
how we're supposed to be dust
and must follow dust to the mighty claymation
in the sky. This isn't that kind of play
anymore, nor are we waiting for Godot or dog
or God or whomever gets dubbed
correct or side-saddled or anything identified.
We can eschew man and woman,
a dusted-up version
of himself-his-highness-royale, and declare
the day itself no-man, as in "I am a Noman," not
a Woman, and carry on with the anxious branding
of Lady Baba's version of Noman hiphop.
This too won't wrap itself in dental floss
with bow ties as a form of speech that might
say something like the death of Kim Jong-Il
comes in threes with Christopher Hitchens
and Vaclav Havel perched in a trinity position.
That is to say, it's not enough
to submit to what noise makes
ambience with how often we breathe
and say the pledge to our electronic equipment –
We can stop using the phrases
of the way the present defines
the past and simply go straight wormhole to magenta
the sunsets so long moved into storage.
Lady Baba wants what she wants, and if you note how,
you'll be saved from the coming salvation
and the past's existential recycling. Did I mention
the fees you'll incur for playing? Not-
Exactly. Signed, one solo band of followers ahead,
Lady Baba.

HAVE A HEART *for Dean Young*

"The heart is the only broken instrument that works."
—T. E. *Kalem*

The accoutrements of quotes. Like a heart,
wear well. Until they turn, shabby, worn down.
Meant to…what? Swell a feeling,
twist the light inside out?
My own, tattered and engorged in shiny hellos,
buttons the eyes of Onward, ho!
My friends have moved, west perhaps.
A heart too turns but not without art-
eries breaking rank, shuffling off
to another coil, another condition.
Did my heart love till now?
One of the hardest parts is words
holed up in a blundering metronome
that can't utter sounds. Gurgle & torment,
until you adjust the one that found you,
took root, implanted a person where your own
once stood. New heart, moving meat
of parts, you send this rush of arterial gaskets
and gush to carnal shores
that suck the soldiers back?
You are the owner of my years, the toll I pay
every next walk or shower I pant to stand in.
I am yours, beloved,
with quotas mutual and a family
I visit where they live. They were always decisions,
not stand-ins, a flesh apart. Some still tell me,
I was the difficult journey, and
"Above all, the idea of death"

carries me across land, then beating waves,
not beaten, toward this thing I call home.
Rivers and roads cradle till I reach you, alone,
in my chest now swelling with what, I can't say.

A ROOM WITHOUT WALLS

Those of us dressed like moonlight know
that good whiskey goes in our heads,
lays us flat in a room without walls.
But if there were walls,
if we were walls,
we'd be the sturdy stand-up kind
so that no one would walk
all over us,
unless Lionel Richie needed
us for a music video for the song,
"Dancing on the Ceiling," which really
means we would be a means to an end,
the end as ceiling. No one looks up
and thinks that's the end,
the ceiling is the end. Even now,
I won't look up. I don't know
if there's a ceiling above or below and
will not invest in such laws of physics.
I want to be beyond walls, the after-walls,
part person, part ethereal star matter,
complete with the engine of lung tissue,
intake valves, computer parts to make
my eyes and ears less fictitious than
what happens in papyrus print
and cotton song. Stuff my orifices,
play a tiny banjo in Spain; I won't let on
I know society-at-large, society in a room
without walls. I can recognize them.
You see, rooms must be smaller
than one imagines, where
the air is tight, to keep productivity

flowing. If the room opens into a field,
the workers wander, walking for miles,
and nothing but motion completes itself.
How can motion finish? Static it isn't.
Is that how we want to sleep in a world,
filled only by the motion of Lionel Richie
walking without walls to get around?
If you think that's enough, the notion
that we should leave rooms without
hindrance, without borders or piers
to guide and keep us from rescuing each other,
then I leave you only with the promise
from a painter unrelated to this place,
one who no longer moves among us, except
along museum walls, in gallery coffins
with "Above all, the idea of death."
—Leonora Carrington

one story

Elizabeth Quinn

FLIGHT

When a voice on the intercom announces that my flight to Atlanta is over-booked, I put away my newspaper, pick up my purse and camera bag, and tell the woman behind the ticket counter that I can be bumped. "Steph," whose nametag wings are crooked and whose index finger lacks a magenta nail, looks up from her computer and frowns.

"I'm sorry Mrs. Baker, but we can't get you to Georgia until tomorrow. Are you sure you want to give up your seat?"

"I'm not in a hurry," I say into my purse, pretending to look for my wallet. But I've already shown my ID to three different people, so it's on top of everything else.

"I know that."

She returns her hands to the keyboard, crunching the buttons faster than my fingers have ever moved to do anything. There's a big black phone in the belly of her desk that she uses to call the a hotel and request a room for a "distressed passenger." She winks at me when she says this, but her voice doesn't waiver from its cool, even tone.

When I pull out my driver's license, it sticks to my military spouse ID and both fall to the counter. Steph picks them up and looks at it, then at me. "Pic-

ture's not so bad." She shakes the fake blonde bangs falling across her left eye and swoops her head closer to mine without pausing her fingers still scurrying across the keyboard.

"These coupons are only $25, but I gave you two. The restaurant's awful, but they'll work at the bar too."

She grins and slides an envelope of papers across the counter. "The hotel's shuttle will pick you up outside baggage claim number four." She leans forward, "I'll be there in," she looks down at her watch, "half an hour."

From the van I make two calls. One to my husband, Mike, who doesn't pick up. He hasn't answered a phone call since he got home from his last tour. He says, "people who've got something to say can leave messages. If they don't, there's no reason for me to get up." He says this from the couch. I tell our machine that the shoot ran over an extra day, hoping maybe he'll remember to feed the dog.

My glass of Cabernet is half-empty when Steph sits down next to me at the bar. I still have $43 on my voucher so I offer to buy her a drink. She unclips her tie, hangs her blazer on the back of her stool, then orders three sidecars. All the magenta nails are gone. Replaced with fire engine red.

"One's for you. Try it," she says to me. "I'll take care of it if it's not your thing." She hoists her purse into her lap and pulls out a voucher envelope just like the one she had given me. "And don't worry about the cash. I got plenty of my own."

Three gulps later, her first drink is gone. She sighs, sits against the back on her stool.

"Four shifts in three days." She drags her

second glass around the first and uses it to bump the empty one to the side. "I have to take off Monday. My son. Kindergarten. It's his first day."

She glances at my left hand. "So, you married in? The military. "

"We're divorced." It just slips out, but I'm glad. "Are you? Married I mean."

All the windows in the restaurant look out onto the parking lot. The safety lights blink on, giving the young night a strange orange hue. "Sort of, " she says.

I try to read her expression but she reaches for her purse and digs out the pack of cigarettes. She lights one, takes a drag. "Where were you headed to, coming from, whatever."

"Atlanta. From Carson City."

"I know. I wrote your ticket. I meant what's your story."

"I work for a magazine. A military promotional thing based in Atlanta." I take a sip of the sidecar, try not to wince, and set the glass down closer to Steph.

I tell her that in Carson City I had to interview Frances Gunderson, a 93 year-old DAR member who founded Operation K-9 Care to send toys to military dogs serving over seas. I also tell her that last month I was sent to Williamsburg, Virginia, and that there I interviewed Hazel Cunningham, a costumed colonial who wrote a book and donated the proceeds to the Organization for Disabled American Veterans. Believing in Butter: The Magic of the Churn.

"And you gave up your seat home for this?" She swings one arm over her head and waves her

hand around like she's trying to stir up the stale air.

I stare at the red stain in the bottom of my glass, then order another.

"The flight coupon."

"It takes more than a coupon to put a person in an airport hotel." Steph reaches for her second sidecar and pushes the extra back towards me. "Take one more sip."

Sliding a laminated cardboard menu across the bar top towards us, she asks, "You hungry? Only thing I've eaten today is a pretzel. You know, one of those giant ones. You like seafood?" To the bartender, "Can we sit at that table by the window?"

We've finished a pound of boiled shrimp, two Caesar salads, half a bottle of Chardonnay, and a conversation about hurricane season in the Gulf when Steph pushes her plates to the empty side of the table and turns her chair and sits back, her whole body facing mine.

"You asked and now I'm going to tell you." She throws the napkin from her lap onto the table. "I married Joe six years ago. He went AWOL. I haven't heard a word from him in three years."

She reaches for her cigarettes and lights one. "We're still technically married." Her drag is hard and deep, like she's sucking in a breath of fresh air.

I don't want to interrupt to tell her I'm sorry. Plus, I can't tell if she is.

"Bummer," I mumble. It sounded okay in my head, but now the word seems awkward in the silence between us. I lift my glass to take a sip but nothing hits my lips.

She takes the glass from my hand, fills it, then empties the bottle into hers, letting it hover, tilted

upright, before setting it back on the table.

"Shit, there must have been a hole in that one," she says, laughing.

Her eyes close when her lips meet her glass, her chest rising towards her chin, pausing, then sinking into place.

"Joe was a bartender. He'd set me up all night long just to keep me there, I mean LITs, martinis, whatever I wanted. He was taking classes but couldn't find anything he was interested in. I was studying drama at UT and was about to graduate. One day he showed up at my apartment, said he'd joined the Army, that he was being sent to basic training and that when he got back, he wanted to get married."

She taps her cigarette on the rim of the ashtray, rests it in one of the notches, then looks up. "I told him the whole thing was stupid. He said he needed the discipline. He said he wouldn't have to fight, that he would just train, serve on the base for a couple of years, then go into the reserves. He'd only been gone three weeks when I found out I was pregnant."

"Oh, Jesus." I put my hand to my mouth.

"That's exactly what I said. I didn't want a kid." She leans into the table. "And he can be the worst little shit, but, I swear, they do something to you that makes you love them."

"It must have been scary. To do it alone."

"I didn't last long. I left school and followed Joe to his station at Fort Hood. We got married, Matt was born. Joe said he liked working in armory, handling the big guns, playing around in the tanks. I wasn't crazy about life on the base. I didn't exactly get along with the other wives."

She lifts her wine glass, as if to clink it against one that's not there, and grins.

"But I loved being a mother. I thought if we could get through the two years he had to serve, we had a chance, happily ever after."

When she picks up her cigarette to relight it, her eyes cross as she stares at the tip until it starts to glow.

"Then the world went crazy." She waves her hand, limp in front of her chest, as if she's trying to shake off an unwanted dampness. "When they sent the 101st from Fort Campbell to Afghanistan, everyone on our base started to panic. When they moved to Iraq, we knew it was only a matter of time."

She looks down into the glass cupped in the palm of her right hand. The shadows from the blinds on the window above our table paint thick black stripes across her face. There's more light outside in the neon of the parking lot than in the restaurant.

"That's awful." I could tell her I was there, at Fort Campbell. I could tell her what I remember about the morning Mike left was that we were out of bread. I wanted a piece of toast but we had no bread. So I got in our car and drove. I didn't stop at the store on the base or even in Clarksville. I just kept driving. Two hours later I hit Nashville. I exited the interstate into the neighborhood where I had lived in college and pulled into the parking lot of the store where I used to shop. When I turned off the car, I looked down and saw that I was still in my nightgown. I wasn't even wearing shoes.

"Until the war, it'd been a game to Joe. He'd enjoyed the training, the machinery, hanging out

with other guys. But when his division was called to serve, I've never seen anyone so freaked out."

She swirls a sip of wine around the edge her glass. "The night before they were supposed to leave, Joe was calmer than he'd been in months. He wanted lasagna for his last supper. We drank two bottles of Chianti, fooled around, watched Letterman, and went to bed. I guess the wine helped me sleep. When I woke up to the alarm, he was gone. Until the officers came to the door, I thought he had just wanted to avoid our good-bye."

"He never said a word? Hasn't tried to call you or anything?"

"A few days later, I found a note. In my underwear drawer. It said how sorry he was and how much he loved me. Bullshit. He wasn't ready for any of it, me or the war."

Steph pours the remainder of her wine down the back of her throat and motions for me to do the same.

"So, that's my sob story. Not too impressive. There's way worse. It gives me an excuse to cut loose every now and then."

She scoots her chair away from the table. "Let's move back to the bar."

When she stands I do too. "Steph, I'm..."

She puts her hand on my shoulder. "Let's get another drink."

While we're walking to the bar, a group wearing slacks and Polo shirts stream into the lounge. Two men still wearing nametags, drinking from plastic cups follow us to the counter. When I prop myself up on the stool, I turn my back so they can't see the heat in my cheeks. Steph grins, sticks her

chest out, and sits with her hips aimed in their direction. Maintaining eye contact with them, she tilts her head towards me and whispers, "They love a girl in uniform."

My shoulders are heavy, my breath metallic. A martini does not make conversation with the Toyota salesmen any more interesting. Steph's laugh is too loud, and my body is limp. When they touch her, they notice how she responds.
"Excuse me," I say. "I'm going to get some fresh air."
"Don't be long, darlin'," Steph grabs my forearm. "I need your young blood."

On the patio by the bean-shaped pool, I take deep breaths of the cool night air. Sharp and milky. Like biting into a cucumber.
The surface of the water catches the lights from the parking lot, throws the pieces back in all sorts of different directions. Pellets fired from a shotgun shell.

I wake up cold and startled. Steph is leaning over me laughing. Backlit by the pool lights, her face is dark and lumpy.
"You trying to ditch me?"
The top two buttons of her blouse are undone, and I can see the red silk of her bra.
I'm stiff and damp, not sure how long I've been asleep. My head feels hollow and my tongue has swollen to the edges of my mouth.
"Come on, sleepy head. I've got a project for you."

I brush my hair out of my face and wipe the damp from my mouth. "What time is it?"

"Early." Steph flings my purse and camera bag into my lap and sits down on the end of my recliner. "I met these men, talent scouts. They said I've got a 'fresh look.' Can you believe that? How old do they think I am?"

"The car salesmen?"

"They went to bed. These guys are younger, really cute. Modeling agents or something. So, anyway, they asked if I had ever posed before, and I said no, but I have a friend who's a photographer and I can start tonight."

She shakes her head, then runs her fingertips through the ends of her hair, brushing large pieces forward to the front of her shoulders. "Luckily I always travel with at least one pair of sexy underwear. Sheer black. And it's got a matching bra."

When she smiles the lines around her face and eyes deepen, seeming richer in the gray light surrounding us.

"So, will you do it? I mean, it could be fun.."

"I don't know. I don't really have any equipment. Just this one lens. No flashes."

Crossing her arms over her chest, Steph juts out her lower lip and furrows her eyebrows so they look like a penciled 'v' pointing towards her powered nose.

"Come on. If you want, I'll do you too." She tugs at one of the tips of my collar. "All you got to do is take off this silly vest and undo a couple of buttons. I got some big silver hoops in my room we can trade for these pearls. You loosen up a bit, you might even be sexier than me."

When she laughs, her breath hits me in the face. It smells like Mike's frat house the morning after a party.

"I need a glass of water." I swing my legs off the recliner, away from Steph, and steady my feet on the ground. When I hang my purse on my shoulder and drape the camera case across my body, Steph grabs for it, but misses.

"Jesus, Annie. Don't be such prude." She unhands the bag, stands. "You married your college sweetheart, right? He went to war. When he got back he was different. Blah blah blah. That shit happens everyday."

When she crosses her arms over her chest, our eyes lock. Neither of us looks away.

The patio door opens behind me. Male voices drift outside. Feet shuffle across the concrete.

"Hey, honey, you coming up or what?"

She drops her arms, rolls back her shoulders so her chest sticks out towards them.

"Be right there," Steph says, straining her voice to an unnaturally high octave.

Her shoulder knocks mine when she shuffles by, smiling at the men, not even looking at me.

"That your photographer friend?"

His breath on my neck hardens my resolve not to turn around.

"We can't all be fun." Before she follows them back inside she turns back to me, whispers, "I bet you used to be."

The *Timmy T's* sign is dark and the lobby is empty except for a young girl behind the desk reading a magazine. Her tie hangs loose around her neck,

her eyelids are painted and heavy. I show her my key and ask for directions to the stairs. When I get to the third floor, I pause on the landing, then collapse on the ground, prop my back against the door.

The clock on my cell phone reads 1:00 am, 3:00 in Atlanta. Zero three-hundred hours at Fort McPherson. No way Mike is up. But I dial anyway, desperate for something familiar, even my voice on our machine.

"Yeah," surprisingly alert voice breaks into the ring tone.

"Mike."

"Annie? Where the hell are you? I went to the airport. They said you didn't get on your flight."

"Omaha." I laugh.

"Do you know how much gas costs right now?"

"I left you a message."

"This isn't funny. Are you drunk?"

I lean my elbow into my thigh, rest my head on my hand. "Mike, I'm tired."

"Then go to sleep."

"It's my stupid job, that awful base, our dirty apartment..." The fluorescent lights in the stairwell exaggerate the bright white walls.

"What are you talking about?" His voice is sharp, angry.

"And you. I'm tired."

"I got my orders today. Iraq. Two weeks."

My eyes open onto a cigarette burn in the patch of carpet underneath my crossed legs. Gray plastic fibers melted black. Exactly the size of the tip of my pointer finger.

"God, when is it going to be over?"

"When we finish the job."

I lean back, straighten my spine against the door. "You don't have to go."

"Why wouldn't I?" he says.

"I don't know."

My room is at the opposite end of the floor, but before I reach it, the ding of the elevator breaks the silence in the hall. I peek around the corner and see Steph step into the corridor. She tucks in her shirt with one hand and balances her heels on the fingertips of the other. She walks away from me, but I can see her shoulders rise and fall while she stands facing her door, pausing to fluff her rumpled hair before opening it and crossing into her room.

<u>one essay</u>

Chris Wong

THE STRUCTURE OF WORKSHOP

Over the past two years the editors of US-POCO BOOKS have made the case in mutiple publications, including print and online venues, that the MFA programs of America comprise a school of poetry, defined largely by the workshop environment. I would like to briefly discuss that environment, and the apparent workshop process itself.

Over the last four years of my life as a student of creative writing, I have sat in a variety of poetry workshops. In these workshops I have read and written poetry that has had formalist, symbolist, confessionalist, experimentalist, and imagistic leanings. How then can I, or any of my classmates, be of a single school? Because the workshop is an all governing scene. I will explain what I mean.

We, insofar as we reason, live simultaneously within myriad structural systems, all of which are overbearing and restrictive in how we see the world. For instance, our understanding of the family structure dictates how even those of us with the most tedious of relatives should feel about Thanksgiving (i.e. thankful) and insures that no matter how rationally we view our absolutely justifiable resentment toward Uncle Ted's overbearing dullness or our Great Aunt Hortense's well-meaning but prying inquiry, we will still feel a certain pang of guilt when we retreat to the

back porch with our bottle of bourbon and cigarette and bear the late November frost rather than spend another minute around that kitchen table. Because they are family, and we understand what family is by what it is supposed to be.

Structures invade us in all spheres of life. For instance, as college students we understand what a college freshman is supposed to look like, listen to, watch on television, and wear and we either conform, rebel, or decide to ignore the choice to conform or rebel. Any such choice is a reaction to this structure. Structures are structures are structures. They are ingrained in us. We learn them and internalize them so quickly that they become nearly impossible to recognize and iterate. We leave college as the person we are, shaped by a structure that no longer exists for us. We are apart from it but it still defines ourselves.

A poetry workshop, it should go without saying, is a structure. One is inundated with rules and procedures in the first meeting of one's first workshop—positive statements should accompany negative statements, no personal attacks are allowed, the author should not respond directly to any criticism except at the end of the session, etc. There are other structures to workshop as well, more unspoken structures governing how participants should interact, whose opinions matter most, and how dialogues should progress through each discussion. However, the structure of workshop I find most relevant and overwhelming is the "public opinion" structure.

In a room of poets, reading each other's work and putting forth their own work, there are necessary and useful currents of resistance at play at all times. One does not bring a work to workshop expecting

universal praise (although one hopes at times). Yet, the fragile or stalwart ego (and id, for that matter) of the poet demands that one react or deliberately not-react to the criticisms one receives in workshop. Like my earlier example of the structure of Thanksgiving, a workshop poet knows rationally that frustrating comments have many understandable origins—stylistic disharmony between the two principles, a lack of careful attention to the poet's choices, a fundamental lack of quality in the poet's work itself. The poet rationally knows that any workshop comment must be taken with a grain of salt. He or she knows this.

However, enough grains of salt can eat away at the sturdiest foundations, given enough time. I don't consider myself particularly susceptible to the opinions of other writers (who does, after all?). Still, at one point in my MFA career I found myself looking down at a particularly dull poem, full of obvious symbols, a contrived narrative, and a complete lack of attention to the music of speech. Revisiting this poem, I couldn't think of anything but the workshop's reaction. "There is nothing in here that could possibly confuse them," I thought, almost despite myself. "They might not like it, but what can they say against it?" As soon as I realized that, I knew it was time to take a stance. To accept the impact of the structure of workshop and come to terms (my own personal terms) with what the response of workshop ingrains into a writer about writing and the act of sharing what is written. The structural governance of the workshop.

Ah. The structure of workshop. This was a low moment in my life and it was owing to workshop and the MFA and any number of other things. But

this is not to criticize the MFA. Quite the opposite. As I said before, when one encounters a structure, one accepts the structure, rebels against the structure, or chooses to ignore the structure. We all, poets, all of us, love poetry. We know what it means to be a poet and we know the inroads and avenues to get there. We can seduce dowagers and live as a recluse. We can jot down poems on the backs of prescription pads. We can meditate on our walks to the agency. We can ride a motorcycle across the country and be poor and drunk and jobless. We can enroll in an MFA program. However at some point the MFA program goes away, the workshop goes away and we are the writers who we are.

    We choose or we do not choose. But every poet is working within a structure. A structure which is both forgiving and unforgiving. Poetry, by its nature is both charitable and merciless. Achingly simple and maddeningly difficult. Everyone teaches him or herself and is taught to write. At one point or another, one must gaze into the labyrinthine matrices that comprise the structural system of poetry and be steeled against whatever it is one steels him or herself against. One must assert one's individual identity if one is to survive as a singular entity in a world that basically has no use for that singular entity. The workshop, it seems, is as good and as bad a forge for that steel. But it is a forge, make no mistake. No more, no less.

USPOCO BOOKS is a division of us poetry company, a constantly touring personal service corp. formed by Chris and Rebecca Pappas on April 1st, 2009 in Fayetteville, AR. *The Road To Nowhere Tour* began on May 29, 2009.

Founded with a group of professors, students and local artists frustrated by the seeming impossibility of useful learning while confined in competing institutional roles, the first members of us poetry company organized to push for curriculum reform at The University of Arkansas in some fairly innovative ways.

The troupe demonstrated what it saw as the new educational model, by writing plays to learn English composition, by using collaborative methods for creating poetry and short fiction to be performed or published on any corner of campus, and by becoming active in a campus movement for general curriculum reform. Some of the students involved went on to found art-centered student groups and literary journals.

Over three years of touring, performing, and teaching, us poetry company has developed an improvisational teaching style for improvisational minds; we are now implementing this new style and new curriculum in community based educational programs, as well as academic based programs.

us poetry company offers teacher enrichment training, business writing courses, camps, and classes in the arts, as well as personalized poetry instruction for all ages.

ManuFactured Artists is a grass roots community of writers working for writers. Email the editors at **uspocobooks@gmail.com** for more info. Or visit us at **uspoco.com** and **ManuFacturedArtists.com**.

Made in the USA
Lexington, KY
23 April 2013